Seymour Simon

KILLER WHALES

SCHOLASTIC INC.
New York Toronto London Auckland Sydney
Mexico City New Delhi Hong Kong Buenos Aires

This book is dedicated to my wife, Joyce.

Special thanks to reading consultant Dr. Linda B. Gambrell, Director of the School of Education at Clemson University, past president of the National Reading Conference, and past board member of the International Reading Association.

Permission to use the following photographs is gratefully acknowledged:
front cover: © Jeanne White, Photo Researchers, Inc.; title page, pages 4–5: © Marilyn Kazmers/Dembinsky Photo Assoc. Inc.; pages 2–3, 10–11: © Tom McHugh, Photo Researchers, Inc.; pages 6–7: © Art Wolfe, Photo Researchers, Inc.; pages 8–9: © Patrick J. Endres/Visuals Unlimited; pages 12–13: © David B. Fleetham/Visuals Unlimited; pages 14–15: © Gregory Ochocki, Photo Researchers, Inc.; pages 16–17, 32: © Tom & Pat Leeson, Photo Researchers, Inc.; pages 18–19: © Tom Myers, Photo Researchers, Inc.; pages 20–21: © Bruce Frisch, Photo Researchers, Inc.; pages 22–23: © George D. Lepages, Photo Researchers, Inc.; pages 24–29: © Brandon Cole; pages 30–31: © Jerry McCormick-Ray, Photo Researchers, Inc.

ISBN 0-439-46683-0

Text copyright 2002 © by Seymour Simon. All rights reserved.
Published by Scholastic Inc., 557 Broadway, New York, NY 10012, by arrangement with North-South Books, Inc. SCHOLASTIC and associated logos are trademarks and/or registered trademarks of Scholastic Inc.

12 11 10 9 8 7 6 5 4 3 2 1   3 4 5 6 7 8/0

Printed in the U.S.A.   23

First Scholastic printing, January 2003

Killer whales are big, fast,

and beautiful.

The large males are bigger than

elephants and as fast as sharks.

Killer whales often leap
clear out of the water.
Killer whales are exciting
to watch and learn about.

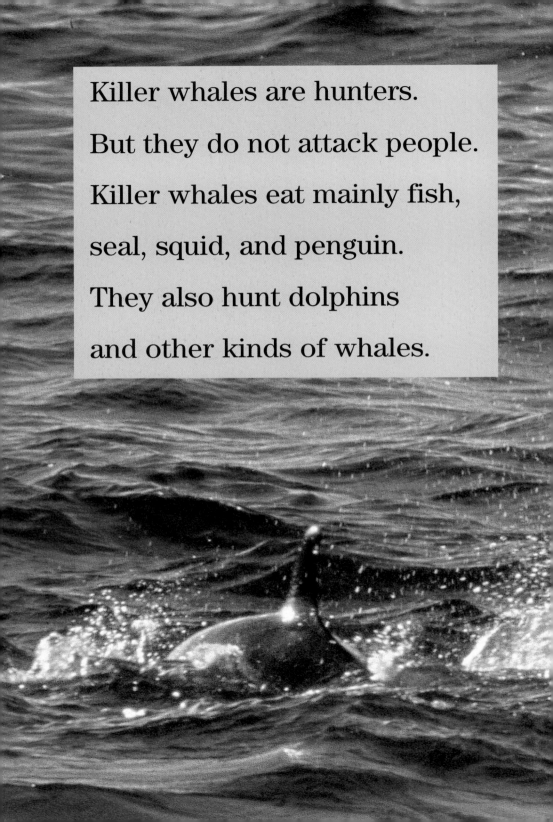

Killer whales are hunters.

But they do not attack people.

Killer whales eat mainly fish,

seal, squid, and penguin.

They also hunt dolphins

and other kinds of whales.

Many people call the killer
whale an orca.

Orca is the name scientists use.

Killer whales are found in
all the oceans of the world.

Most of them live in
the icy waters around
the North or South poles.

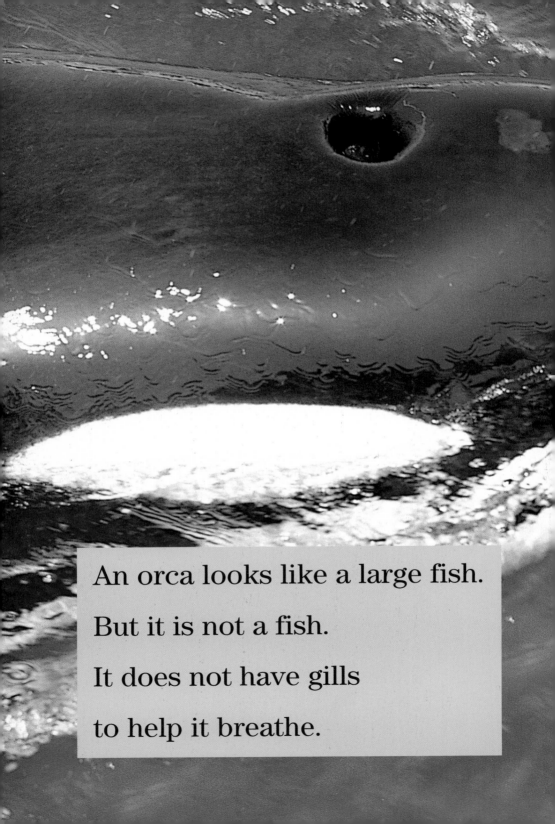

An orca looks like a large fish.

But it is not a fish.

It does not have gills

to help it breathe.

Instead, an orca breathes through
a blowhole on the top of its head.
And it has lungs like dogs,
cats, and people.
An orca can hold its breath
for ten minutes or longer.

A female orca is nearly 20 feet long.

That's as long as an ambulance.

A male orca is a few feet longer.

It weighs up to ten tons.

That's as heavy as two elephants.

Orcas are good swimmers.
They can move through the
water at 30 miles per hour.
That's faster than you can run.

Orcas use their tails,
called flukes, for power.
They use flippers to steer
and to turn.

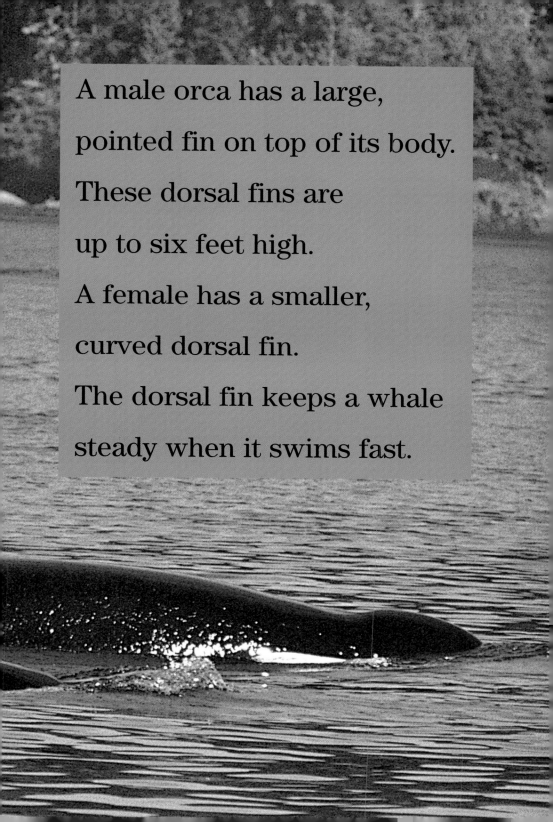

A male orca has a large,
pointed fin on top of its body.
These dorsal fins are
up to six feet high.
A female has a smaller,
curved dorsal fin.
The dorsal fin keeps a whale
steady when it swims fast.

In dark or cloudy waters, orcas
make special clicking sounds.
Then they listen to the way
the sounds echo back.

This lets the orcas know
what is around them.

Orcas have sharp, three-inch-long teeth for hunting.

Like wolves, orcas hunt in packs. They circle and herd their prey before attacking.

Orcas live in family groups called pods.
The members of a pod hunt and feed together.
They protect one another.

Some pods have fewer
than 10 whales.
Other pods have as many
as 50 whales.

Female orcas are called cows.
Male orcas are called bulls.
Baby orcas are born under
water, near the surface.

A newborn orca calf

is eight feet long.

It weighs nearly 400 pounds.

A mother orca
nurses its calf
with milk.
Calves begin eating fish
and other foods at about
four months of age.
In one year the calf will grow
to be ten feet long and weigh
more than 1,000 pounds.

Orcas can leap high into the air.
Then they land back in the water
with a big SPLASH!
This is called breaching.

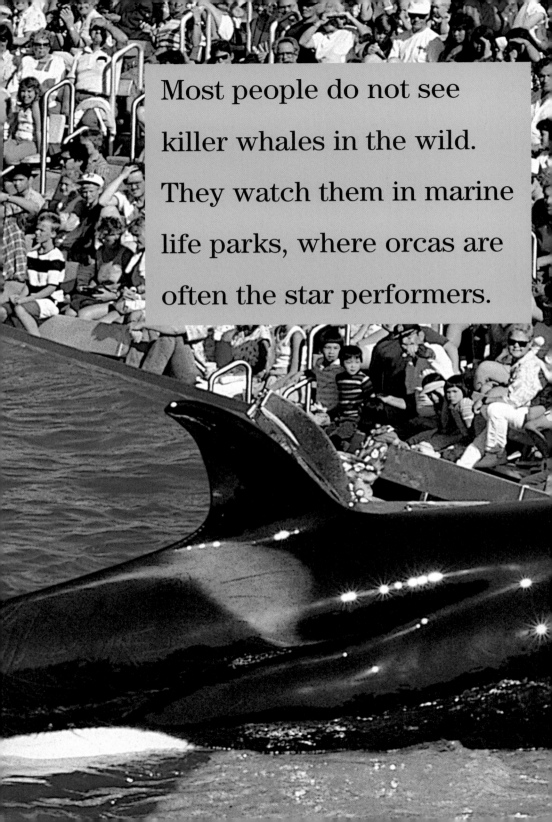

Most people do not see killer whales in the wild. They watch them in marine life parks, where orcas are often the star performers.

Scientists also study orcas in these parks.
They have found that orcas learn quickly.

Much about orcas remains a mystery. But as we learn more about orcas, we gain a better understanding of all wild animals.